W9-AJT-535

WHERE DO CATS LIVE?

Ron Hirschi

Photographs by
Linda Quartman Younker

Walker and Company
New York

For Bleu, Pippins, Buster, and Cindy, too!   R. H.
For Muriel and Razzmatazz   L. Q. Y.

First published in the United States of America in 1991
by Walker Publishing Company, Inc.

Published simultaneously in Canada by Thomas Allen & Son
Canada, Limited, Markham, Ontario

Library of Congress Cataloging-in-Publication Data
Hirschi, Ron.
Where do cats live? / Ron Hirschi: photographs by Linda Quartman Younker.
p.   cm.
Summary: Brief text and photographs present the places where both wild and domestic cats live.
ISBN 0-8027-8109-8 (trade).—ISBN 0-8027-8110-1 (rein)
1. Cats—Juvenile literature.   2. Cats—Habitat—Juvenile
literature. [1. Cats—Habitat.] I. Younker, Linda Quartman, ill. II. Title.
SF445.7.H58   1991
599.74'428'045—dc20   91-15421
CIP
AC

PRINTED IN HONG KONG

2 4 6 8 10 9 7 5 3 1

Cats live with cat lovers

with old sweaters for beds,

warm friendly laps,

and bowls of fresh milk to drink
just before afternoon naps.

Cats live with one another,

on lonely, cold streets,

and out in the darkness where
wild and tame meet.

Cats live in barns,

on boats,

and in stores.

Cats live with your grandmother,

and, when no homes can be found, cats live in the pound.

Cats live where birds try to hide

from sharp claws and
pouncing paws

and up in the window where
watching is best.

Cats have lived with people for centuries, but they have lived in the wild for many more thousands of years. Domestic cats seem to hold on to their wildness in the ways they show their independence, their need to chase birds, and in their sleek stalking movements before they pounce. But tame cats are truly dependent on people for all their basic survival needs.

Sadly, adult cats and many kittens are a large part of the more than 13 million unwanted animals put to death each year. You can help stop this needless problem by having your male cat neutered or your female cat spayed. There are plenty of unwanted kittens and cats in the world, and one way to show your love for these animals is to have your own cat fixed.

In making a happy home for your cat, think also of the needs of the truly wild cougars, jaguars, bobcats, ocelots, and other cat relatives. Look into your cat's eyes and think of the special habitat needs of these American cats of forest and mountain. Learn as much as you can about all the places where cats live. Like your own cat friend, they will survive only if you take the time to help protect their homes.